Grammaropolis
PRESENTS

WONDERFUL WORDS
FOR FIFTH GRADE

VOCABULARY AND WRITING WORKBOOK

BY ORDER OF

The Mayor of Grammaropolis

Written by Christopher Knight
Interior Design by Christopher Knight
Cover Design by Mckee Frazior
Grammaropolis Character Design by Powerhouse Animation & Mckee Frazior

ISBN: 9781644420553
Copyright © 2021 by Grammaropolis LLC
All rights reserved.
Published by Six Foot Press
Printed in the U.S.A.

Grammaropolis.com
SixFootPress.com

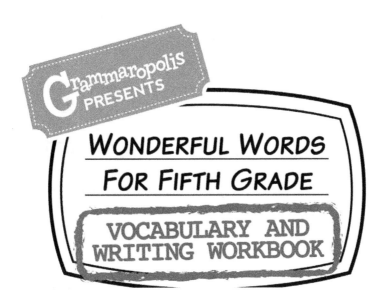

Grammaropolis
PRESENTS

WONDERFUL WORDS
FOR FIFTH GRADE

VOCABULARY AND WRITING WORKBOOK

GRAMMAROPOLIS BOOKS

HOUSTON

FROM THE DESK OF THE MAYOR

Greetings, fellow wordsmith!

Thank you so much for using this workbook. I hope you have fun learning some new vocabulary words!

As you know, many words can act as multiple parts of speech; it all depends on how they're used in the sentence. For the sake of clarity and simplicity (and because we didn't have enough space on the page!), the definitions in this workbook include only one part of speech for each word.

It's great to know a lot of vocabulary words, but the real reason we expand our vocabulary is so that we can communicate more effectively. That's why I've added a writing exercise, with optional prompts, at the end of each section.

Thanks again for visiting Grammaropolis. I hope you enjoy your stay!

—The Mayor

TABLE OF CONTENTS

How to Use the Vocabulary Pages

SYLLABLE BREAKDOWN

PHONETIC PRONUNCIATION

DICTIONARY PRONUNCIATION

PART OF SPEECH

foofaraw

foo·fa·raw • [FOO-fuh-raw] • \ ˈfü-fə-ˌrȯ \

- **noun**
  1. a great fuss or disturbance about something insignificant

My sister made a big **foofaraw** when I told her that someone had scratched her car, but I think she totally overreacted.

USAGE EXAMPLE IN A COMPLETE SENTENCE

DICTIONARY DEFINITION

SYNONYM

ANTONYM

excitement

indifference

WRITE YOUR OWN ANTONYM HERE

WRITE YOUR OWN SYNONYM HERE

Writing Time!
Use *foofaraw* in an original sentence of your own creation.

Last night at dinner my cat knocked over a glass of water and caused a real foofaraw.

PRACTICE USING THE WORD BY WRITING AN ORIGINAL SENTENCE

Bonus Fun Time!
Express *foofaraw* with a drawing or invent a dictionary-style definition of your own.

INVENT A DEFINITION

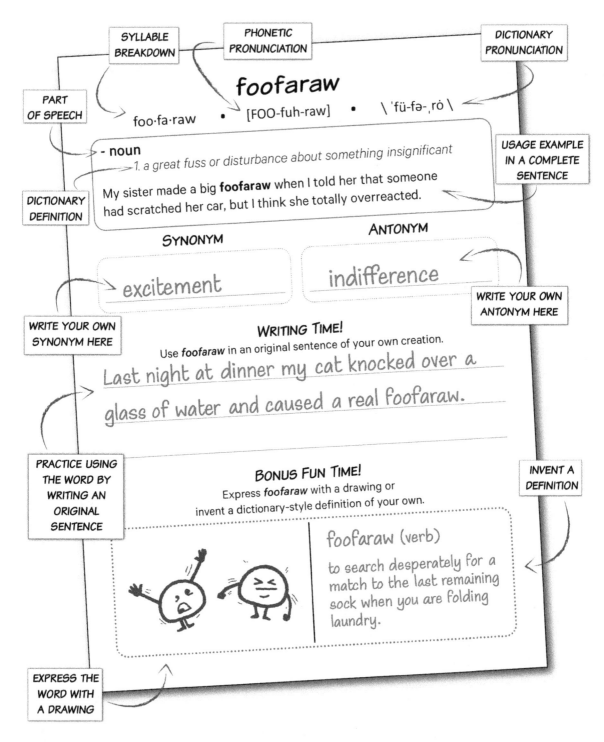

foofaraw (verb)

to search desperately for a match to the last remaining sock when you are folding laundry.

EXPRESS THE WORD WITH A DRAWING

Important Note: Synonyms and antonyms for nouns might be harder to come up with than they are for verbs and adjectives, but do your best!

THE PARTS OF SPEECH REVIEW

Every word acts as at least one of the eight parts of speech. In this workbook, you'll find nouns, verbs, and adjectives. Here are some things you need to remember about them!

NOUNS

A noun can name a person, place, thing, or idea.

Naming a person:
Jason is my very best **friend**.

Naming a place:
Becks Prime is my favorite **restaurant**.

Naming a thing:
That **ball** is my favorite **toy**.

Naming an idea:
Honesty and **loyalty** are my best **qualities**.

VERBS

An action verb expresses mental or physical action, and a linking verb expresses a state of being.

Expressing physical action:
Richard **jumped** across the river.

Expressing mental action:
Richard **considered** jumping across the river.

Expressing a state of being:
Richard **feels** bad. He **is** sorry for jumping across the river.

ADJECTIVES

*An adjective modifies a noun or a pronoun and tells **what kind, which one, how much,** or **how many.***

Modifying a noun:
The **quick brown** fox jumped over the **enormous red** fence at the **first** sign of trouble.

Modifying a pronoun:
They are **satisfied** with the answer, but I am still **curious**.

There are five other parts of speech you won't find in this workbook, but that doesn't mean they're not important!

ADVERBS

*An adverb modifies a verb, an adjective, or another adverb and tells **how, where, when,** or **to what extent.***

PRONOUNS

A pronoun takes the place of one or more nouns or pronouns.

PREPOSITIONS

A preposition shows a logical relationship or locates an object in time or space.

CONJUNCTIONS

A conjunction joins words or word groups.

INTERJECTIONS

An interjection expresses strong or mild emotion.

SECTION ONE: WORD PREVIEW
Welcome to your ten new favorite words!

When you encounter a new word, take a moment to consider what it might mean.

1. Think about the word and circle what part of speech you think it is.
   *(Many words can act as more than one part of speech, depending on how they're used in the sentence, **so only choose one part of speech below**.)*
2. Come up with a brief definition of the word in the part of speech you've chosen. It doesn't have to be the *correct* definition—just do your best.

captivity
Part of Speech: noun   verb   adjective

Definition:_____

_____

mock
Part of Speech: noun   verb   adjective

Definition:_____

_____

effortless
Part of Speech: noun   verb   adjective

Definition:_____

_____

peer
Part of Speech: noun   verb   adjective

Definition:_____

_____

address
Part of Speech: noun   verb   adjective

Definition:_____

_____

unfamiliar
Part of Speech: noun   verb   adjective

Definition:_____

_____

concentrate
Part of Speech: noun   verb   adjective

Definition:_____

_____

request
Part of Speech: noun   verb   adjective

Definition:_____

_____

circular
Part of Speech: noun   verb   adjective

Definition:_____

_____

precious
Part of Speech: noun   verb   adjective

Definition:_____

_____

captivity

cap·tiv·i·ty • [kap-tIv-uh-tee] • \ kap-ˈti-və-tē \

> **- noun**
>
> *1. the condition of being imprisoned or confined*
>
> Polar bears may be happier in the wild than they are in **captivity**.

SYNONYM

ANTONYM

WRITING TIME!
Use *captivity* in an original sentence of your own creation.

BONUS FUN TIME!
Express *captivity* with a drawing, or
invent a dictionary-style definition of your own.

mock

mock   •   [mAHk]   •   \ ˈmäk \

- verb
1. to treat with scorn or contempt or ridicule;
2. to make a sham of

Monica got in trouble when she **mocked** her little sister.

SYNONYM

ANTONYM

WRITING TIME!
Use *mock* in an original sentence of your own creation.

BONUS FUN TIME!
Express *mock* with a drawing, or
invent a dictionary-style definition of your own.

effortless

ef·fort·less   •   [Ef-uhrt-luhs]   •   \ ˈefərtləs \

- adjective

  1. requiring no physical or mental exertion

Climbing trees is hard for some people, but for me it's **effortless**.

SYNONYM

ANTONYM

WRITING TIME!
Use *effortless* in an original sentence of your own creation.

BONUS FUN TIME!
Express *effortless* with a drawing, or
invent a dictionary-style definition of your own.

peer

peer • [pIR] • \ ˈpir \

> **- noun**
>
> *1. one that is of the same or equal standing (as in law, rank, quality, age, ability) with another*
>
> We all got together with our **peers** in class and voted on what to do.

SYNONYM

ANTONYM

WRITING TIME!

Use *peer* in an original sentence of your own creation.

BONUS FUN TIME!

Express *peer* with a drawing, or
invent a dictionary-style definition of your own.

address

ad·dress   •   [uh-drEs]   •   \ ə-'dres \

- verb
  1. to make straight : set in order;
  2. to communicate directly

Please look me in the eye when you **address** me, okay?

SYNONYM

ANTONYM

WRITING TIME!
Use *address* in an original sentence of your own creation.

_____

_____

_____

BONUS FUN TIME!
Express *address* with a drawing, or
invent a dictionary-style definition of your own.

unfamiliar

un·fa·mil·iar   •   [uhn-fuh-mIl-yuhr]   •   \ ˌən-fə-ˈmil-yər \

- **adjective**
  1. *not well known : strange, unaccustomed;*
  2. *not well acquainted*

That new television show is **unfamiliar** to me, but Sandra has seen it.

SYNONYM

ANTONYM

WRITING TIME!
Use *unfamiliar* in an original sentence of your own creation.

BONUS FUN TIME!
Express *unfamiliar* with a drawing, or
invent a dictionary-style definition of your own.

concentrate

con·cen·trate • [kAHn-suhn-trayt] • \ ˈkän(t)-sən-ˌtrāt \

- verb

1. to focus one's mental effort on a particular object or activity;
2. to render less dilute or diffuse

I **concentrated** on my homework even though the baby was crying.

SYNONYM

ANTONYM

WRITING TIME!

Use *concentrate* in an original sentence of your own creation.

BONUS FUN TIME!

Express *concentrate* with a drawing, or
invent a dictionary-style definition of your own.

request

re·quest • [ri-kwEst] • \ ri-ˈkwest \

- verb

1. to ask (as a person or an organization) to do something;

2. to express a wish or desire (to do something)

You must request an **extension** from your teacher for that project.

SYNONYM

ANTONYM

WRITING TIME!

Use *request* in an original sentence of your own creation.

_____

_____

_____

BONUS FUN TIME!

Express *request* with a drawing, or
invent a dictionary-style definition of your own.

circular

cir·cu·lar • [sUHR-kyuh-luhr] • \ ˈsər-kyə-lər \

- adjective
   1. having the exact or approximate form or outline of a circle;
   2. marked by motion in a circle

A flat, **circular** stone is easier to skip across a lake.

SYNONYM

ANTONYM

WRITING TIME!
Use *circular* in an original sentence of your own creation.

BONUS FUN TIME!
Express *circular* with a drawing, or
invent a dictionary-style definition of your own.

precious

pre·cious   •   [prEsh-uhs]   •   \ ˈpre-shəs \

- adjective

    1. of great value or high price;
    2. very highly esteemed or cherished

The treasure chest was filled with rubies and other **precious** gems.

SYNONYM

ANTONYM

WRITING TIME!
Use *precious* in an original sentence of your own creation.

BONUS FUN TIME!
Express *precious* with a drawing, or
invent a dictionary-style definition of your own.

SECTION ONE: WORD REVIEW

Congratulations on learning ten amazing new words! Remember that the whole point of learning new vocabulary is actually to use it, so let's put your new vocabulary to use.

1. Review the words you've learned. Consider what ideas come to mind when you say the words. How about when you read the definitions?
2. Circle at least **two** of your favorites. You'll get to use these when you write your very own story!

captivity — noun
1. the condition of being imprisoned or confined

mock — verb
1. to treat with scorn or contempt or ridicule;
2. to make a sham of

effortless — adjective
1. requiring no physical or mental exertion

peer — noun
1. one that is of the same or equal standing (as in law, rank, quality, age, ability) with another

address — verb
1. to make straight : set in order;
2. to communicate directly

unfamiliar — adjective
1. not well known : strange, unaccustomed;
2. not well acquainted

concentrate — verb
1. to focus one's mental effort on a particular object or activity;
2. to render less dilute or diffuse

request — verb
1. to ask (as a person or an organization) to do something;
2. to express a wish or desire (to do something)

circular — adjective
1. having the exact or approximate form or outline of a circle;
2. marked by motion in a circle

precious — adjective
1. of great value or high price;
2. very highly esteemed or cherished

STORY ONE

1. List the words you've chosen:

_____

2. Write a story that incorporates all of your chosen words. If you can't think of anything to write about, consider these suggestions:
   - **Write a story about the search for buried treasure.**
   - **Write a story that features at least one talking animal.**

Title: _____

_____

_____

_____

_____

_____

_____

_____

Caption: _____

_____

_____

_____

_____

_____

_____

_____

_____

SECTION TWO: WORD PREVIEW
Welcome to your ten new favorite words!

When you encounter a new word, take a moment to consider what it might mean.

1. Think about the word and circle what part of speech you think it is.
   (Many words can act as more than one part of speech, depending on how they're used in the sentence, **so only choose one part of speech below.**)
2. Come up with a brief definition of the word in the part of speech you've chosen. It doesn't have to be the *correct* definition—just do your best.

approval
Part of Speech: noun   verb   adjective

Definition:_____

_____

dissatisfied
Part of Speech: noun   verb   adjective

Definition:_____

_____

humble
Part of Speech: noun   verb   adjective

Definition:_____

_____

significant
Part of Speech: noun   verb   adjective

Definition:_____

_____

ascend
Part of Speech: noun   verb   adjective

Definition:_____

_____

appropriate
Part of Speech: noun   verb   adjective

Definition:_____

_____

investigate
Part of Speech: noun   verb   adjective

Definition:_____

_____

ordinary
Part of Speech: noun   verb   adjective

Definition:_____

_____

familiar
Part of Speech: noun   verb   adjective

Definition:_____

_____

lack
Part of Speech: noun   verb   adjective

Definition:_____

_____

approval

ap·prov·al • [uh-prOO-vuhl] • \ ə-ˈprü-vəl \

- **noun**
  1. the action of approving something;
  2. certification as to acceptability

I always seek my father's **approval** before I ride my bike that far.

SYNONYM

ANTONYM

WRITING TIME!
Use *approval* in an original sentence of your own creation.

BONUS FUN TIME!
Express *approval* with a drawing, or
invent a dictionary-style definition of your own.

dissatisfied

dis·sat·is·fied   •   [dis-sAt-uhs-fied]   •   \ di(s)ˈsadəsˌfīd \

- adjective

1. not pleased or satisfied

Hector liked the menu, but Gabriel was **dissatisfied** with the options.

SYNONYM

ANTONYM

WRITING TIME!
Use *dissatisfied* in an original sentence of your own creation.

BONUS FUN TIME!
Express *dissatisfied* with a drawing, or
invent a dictionary-style definition of your own.

humble

hum·ble   •   [hUHm-buhl]   •   \ ˈhəm-bəl \

- adjective

1. *modest or meek in spirit, manner, or appearance;*
2. *ranking low in the social or political scale*

You should be more **humble** instead of bragging all the time.

SYNONYM

ANTONYM

WRITING TIME!
Use *humble* in an original sentence of your own creation.

BONUS FUN TIME!
Express *humble* with a drawing, or
invent a dictionary-style definition of your own.

significant

sig·nif·i·cant   •   [sig-nIf-i-kuhnt]   •   \ sig-ˈni-fi-kənt \

- adjective
1. having or likely to have influence or effect;
2. having meaning

Al thought the win was **significant**, but I didn't think it mattered.

SYNONYM

ANTONYM

WRITING TIME!
Use *significant* in an original sentence of your own creation.

BONUS FUN TIME!
Express *significant* with a drawing, or
invent a dictionary-style definition of your own.

ascend

as·cend • [uh-sEnd] • \ ˈə-ˈsend \

- verb
1. *to move upward;*
2. *to go up, sometimes by stages with gradual motion*

Carlos **ascended** the ladder carefully so he wouldn't slip and fall.

SYNONYM

ANTONYM

WRITING TIME!
Use *ascend* in an original sentence of your own creation.

BONUS FUN TIME!
Express *ascend* with a drawing, or
invent a dictionary-style definition of your own.

appropriate

ap·pro·pri·ate • [uh-prOH-pree-uht] • \ ə-ˈprō-prē-ət \

- adjective

1. correct or suitable for some purpose or situation

A screwdriver is not an **appropriate** tool when all you have is nails.

SYNONYM

ANTONYM

WRITING TIME!

Use *appropriate* in an original sentence of your own creation.

BONUS FUN TIME!

Express *appropriate* with a drawing, or
invent a dictionary-style definition of your own.

investigate

in·ves·ti·gate • [in-vEs-tuh-gayt] • \ ən'vestə͟gāt \

- **verb**
    1. to observe or study closely;
    2. to inquire into systematically

We **investigated** the possible causes of my cake's disappearance.

SYNONYM

ANTONYM

WRITING TIME!
Use *investigate* in an original sentence of your own creation.

BONUS FUN TIME!
Express *investigate* with a drawing, or
invent a dictionary-style definition of your own.

ordinary

or·di·nary   •   [OR-duh-nair-ee]   •   \ ˈȯr-də-ˌner-ē \

- adjective
> *1. occurring or encountered in the usual course of events;*
> *2. not uncommon or exceptional*

Quinn thinks his action figure is special, but I think it's just **ordinary**.

SYNONYM

ANTONYM

WRITING TIME!
Use *ordinary* in an original sentence of your own creation.

BONUS FUN TIME!
Express *ordinary* with a drawing, or
invent a dictionary-style definition of your own.

familiar

fa·mil·iar • [fuh-mIl-yuhr] • \ fə-ˈmil-yər \

- adjective

1. *well acquainted through personal knowledge or study;*
2. *closely associated*

Are you **familiar** with the *Legends of Tomorrow*?

SYNONYM

ANTONYM

WRITING TIME!
Use *familiar* in an original sentence of your own creation.

BONUS FUN TIME!
Express *familiar* with a drawing, or
invent a dictionary-style definition of your own.

lack

lack • [lAk] • \ ˈlak \

- noun

1. the fact or state of being wanting or deficient

Why do I have a **lack** of candy when other kids have so much of it?

SYNONYM

ANTONYM

WRITING TIME!
Use *lack* in an original sentence of your own creation.

_____

_____

_____

BONUS FUN TIME!
Express *lack* with a drawing, or
invent a dictionary-style definition of your own.

SECTION TWO: WORD REVIEW

Congratulations on learning ten amazing new words! Remember that the whole point of learning new vocabulary is actually to use it, so let's put your new vocabulary to use.

1. Review the words you've learned. Consider what ideas come to mind when you say the words. How about when you read the definitions?
2. Circle at least **two** of your favorites. You'll get to use these when you write your very own story!

approval —— noun
1. the action of approving something;
2. certification as to acceptability

dissatisfied —— adjective
1. not pleased or satisfied

humble —— adjective
1. modest or meek in spirit, manner, or appearance;
2. ranking low in the social or political scale

significant —— adjective
1. having or likely to have influence or effect;
2. having meaning

ascend —— verb
1. to move upward;
2. to go up, sometimes by stages with gradual motion

appropriate —— adjective
1. correct or suitable for some purpose or situation

investigate —— verb
1. to observe or study closely;
2. to inquire into systematically

ordinary —— adjective
1. occurring or encountered in the usual course of events;
2. not uncommon or exceptional

familiar —— adjective
1. well acquainted through personal knowledge or study;
2. closely associated

lack —— noun
1. the fact or state of being wanting or deficient

STORY TWO

1. List the words you've chosen:

_____

2. Write a story that incorporates all of your chosen words. If you can't think of anything to write about, consider these suggestions:
   - **Write a story about a time when you felt extremely happy.**
   - **Write a story in that takes place on the first day of work at your dream job.**

Title: _____

_____

_____

_____

_____

_____

_____

_____

Caption: _____

_____

_____

_____

_____

_____

_____

_____

_____

SECTION THREE: WORD PREVIEW
Welcome to your ten new favorite words!

When you encounter a new word, take a moment to consider what it might mean.

1. Think about the word and circle what part of speech you think it is.
   (Many words can act as more than one part of speech, depending on how they're used in the sentence, **so only choose one part of speech below.**)
2. Come up with a brief definition of the word in the part of speech you've chosen. It doesn't have to be the *correct* definition—just do your best.

hilarious
Part of Speech: noun   verb   adjective

Definition:_____

heroic
Part of Speech: noun   verb   adjective

Definition:_____

variety
Part of Speech: noun   verb   adjective

Definition:_____

benefit
Part of Speech: noun   verb   adjective

Definition:_____

gigantic
Part of Speech: noun   verb   adjective

Definition:_____

argument
Part of Speech: noun   verb   adjective

Definition:_____

descend
Part of Speech: noun   verb   adjective

Definition:_____

apparent
Part of Speech: noun   verb   adjective

Definition:_____

culture
Part of Speech: noun   verb   adjective

Definition:_____

attentive
Part of Speech: noun   verb   adjective

Definition:_____

hilarious

hi·lar·i·ous • [hi-lAIR-ee-uhs] • \ hi-ˈler-ē-əs \

- adjective
  1. extremely amusing;
  2. marked by hilarity

If I tell you a **hilarious** joke, you're going to laugh out loud.

SYNONYM

ANTONYM

WRITING TIME!
Use *hilarious* in an original sentence of your own creation.

BONUS FUN TIME!
Express *hilarious* with a drawing, or
invent a dictionary-style definition of your own.

heroic

he·ro·ic • [hi-rOH-ik] • \ hi-ˈrō-ik \

- adjective

1. having the characteristics of a hero or heroine : very brave

Saving that bird's life was an extremely **heroic** thing to do.

SYNONYM

ANTONYM

WRITING TIME!
Use *heroic* in an original sentence of your own creation.

BONUS FUN TIME!
Express *heroic* with a drawing, or
invent a dictionary-style definition of your own.

variety

va·ri·e·ty • [vuhr-rIE-uh-tee] • \ və-ˈrī-ə-tē \

- noun
1. *the quality or state of being different or diverse;*
2. *something differing from others of the same general kind*

I prefer a **variety** of candies, but Benjamin only likes Milk Duds.

SYNONYM

ANTONYM

WRITING TIME!
Use *variety* in an original sentence of your own creation.

BONUS FUN TIME!
Express *variety* with a drawing, or
invent a dictionary-style definition of your own.

benefit

ben·e·fit • [bEn-uh-fit] • \ ˈbe-nə-ˌfit \

> **- verb**
>
> *1. to be useful, helpful, or profitable to*
>
> Practicing hard will **benefit** you when it comes to playing the game.

SYNONYM

ANTONYM

WRITING TIME!
Use *benefit* in an original sentence of your own creation.

BONUS FUN TIME!
Express *benefit* with a drawing, or
invent a dictionary-style definition of your own.

gigantic

gi·gan·tic   •   [jie-gAn-tik]   •   \ jī'gan(t)ik \

- adjective

1. of very great size or extent : huge or enormous

Cal tried unsuccessfully to fit the **gigantic** burger into his mouth.

SYNONYM

ANTONYM

WRITING TIME!

Use *gigantic* in an original sentence of your own creation.

_____

_____

_____

BONUS FUN TIME!

Express *gigantic* with a drawing, or
invent a dictionary-style definition of your own.

argument

ar·gu·ment • [AHR-gyuh-muhnt] • \ ˈär-gyə-mənt \

- noun
1. an exchange of diverging views, typically heated or angry;
2. a reason given for or against a matter under discussion

We always have the same **argument** about whose style is cooler.

SYNONYM

ANTONYM

WRITING TIME!
Use *argument* in an original sentence of your own creation.

BONUS FUN TIME!
Express *argument* with a drawing, or
invent a dictionary-style definition of your own.

descend

de·scend   •   [di-sEnd]   •   \ dəˈsend \

- **verb**

  1. to go or come down

  Juliet **descended** the staircase to get to the bottom floor.

SYNONYM

ANTONYM

WRITING TIME!

Use *descend* in an original sentence of your own creation.

BONUS FUN TIME!

Express *descend* with a drawing, or
invent a dictionary-style definition of your own.

apparent

ap·par·ent • [uh-pAIR-uhnt] • \ ə-ˈper-ənt \

- adjective
  1. clearly visible or understood;
  2. seeming real or true

There's no **apparent** cause of my sadness; I'm just sad.

SYNONYM

ANTONYM

WRITING TIME!
Use *apparent* in an original sentence of your own creation.

BONUS FUN TIME!
Express *apparent* with a drawing, or
invent a dictionary-style definition of your own.

culture

cul·ture • [kUHl-chuhr] • \ ˈkəl-chər \

> **- noun**
> *1. the artistic expression, attitudes, and behavior characteristic of a particular nation, people, or other social group*
>
> I spent time in Chile, where I learned all about Chilean **culture**.

SYNONYM

ANTONYM

WRITING TIME!

Use *culture* in an original sentence of your own creation.

BONUS FUN TIME!

Express *culture* with a drawing, or
invent a dictionary-style definition of your own.

attentive

at·ten·tive • [uh-tEn-tiv] • \ ə-ˈten-tiv \

- adjective
   1. regarding with care or attention;
   2. heedful or observant

If you want to be a good babysitter, you have to be **attentive**.

SYNONYM

ANTONYM

WRITING TIME!
Use *attentive* in an original sentence of your own creation.

BONUS FUN TIME!
Express *attentive* with a drawing, or
invent a dictionary-style definition of your own.

Section Three: Word Review

Congratulations on learning ten amazing new words! Remember that the whole point of learning new vocabulary is actually to use it, so let's put your new vocabulary to use.

1. Review the words you've learned. Consider what ideas come to mind when you say the words. How about when you read the definitions?
2. Circle at least *two* of your favorites. You'll get to use these when you write your very own story!

hilarious ——— adjective
1. extremely amusing;
2. marked by hilarity

heroic ——— adjective
1. having the characteristics of a hero or heroine : very brave

variety ——— noun
1. the quality or state of being different or diverse;
2. something differing from others of the same general kind

benefit ——— verb
1. to be useful, helpful, or profitable to

gigantic ——— adjective
1. of very great size or extent : huge or enormous

argument ——— noun
1. an exchange of diverging views, typically heated or angry;
2. a reason given for or against a matter under discussion

descend ——— verb
1. to go or come down

apparent ——— adjective
1. clearly visible or understood;
2. seeming real or true

culture ——— noun
1. the artistic expression, attitudes, and behavior characteristic of a particular nation, people, or other social group

attentive ——— adjective
1. regarding with care or attention;
2. heedful or observant

STORY THREE

1. List the words you've chosen:

_____

2. Write a story that incorporates all of your chosen words. If you can't think of anything to write about, consider these suggestions:
   - **Write a story in which the main character is allergic to laughter.**
   - **Write a story in that starts with you bringing a creature (*any creature*) back from extinction.**

Title: _____

_____

_____

_____

_____

_____

_____

_____

_____

Caption: _____

_____

_____

_____

_____

_____

_____

_____

_____

SECTION FOUR: WORD PREVIEW
Welcome to your ten new favorite words!

When you encounter a new word, take a moment to consider what it might mean.
1. Think about the word and circle what part of speech you think it is.
   *(Many words can act as more than one part of speech, depending on how they're used in the sentence, **so only choose one part of speech below.**)*
2. Come up with a brief definition of the word in the part of speech you've chosen. It doesn't have to be the *correct* definition—just do your best.

anxious
Part of Speech: noun   verb   adjective

Definition:_____

_____

express
Part of Speech: noun   verb   adjective

Definition:_____

_____

alert
Part of Speech: noun   verb   adjective

Definition:_____

_____

escalate
Part of Speech: noun   verb   adjective

Definition:_____

_____

exhaust
Part of Speech: noun   verb   adjective

Definition:_____

_____

scarcity
Part of Speech: noun   verb   adjective

Definition:_____

_____

influence
Part of Speech: noun   verb   adjective

Definition:_____

_____

superior
Part of Speech: noun   verb   adjective

Definition:_____

_____

vertical
Part of Speech: noun   verb   adjective

Definition:_____

_____

survive
Part of Speech: noun   verb   adjective

Definition:_____

_____

anxious

anx·ious　　•　　[AngkshUHs]　　•　　\ ˈaŋ(k)-shəs \

- adjective
> *1. characterized by extreme uneasiness of mind;*
> *2. characterized by strong earnest desire : ardently wishing*

I get **anxious** whenever I see a storm cloud on the horizon.

SYNONYM

_____

ANTONYM

_____

WRITING TIME!

Use *anxious* in an original sentence of your own creation.

_____

_____

_____

BONUS FUN TIME!

Express *anxious* with a drawing, or
invent a dictionary-style definition of your own.

express

ex·press • [ik-sprEs] • \ ik'spres \

> **- verb**
>
> *1. to convey (a thought or feeling) in words or by gestures and conduct*
>
> Veronica **expressed** her frustration by stomping up and down.

SYNONYM

ANTONYM

WRITING TIME!
Use *express* in an original sentence of your own creation.

BONUS FUN TIME!
Express *express* (ha ha!) with a drawing, or
invent a dictionary-style definition of your own.

alert

a·lert   •   [uh-lUHRt]   •   \ ə-ˈlərt \

- verb

1. to call to a state of readiness

I will **alert** the fire department if I see the slightest sign of smoke.

SYNONYM

ANTONYM

WRITING TIME!

Use *alert* in an original sentence of your own creation.

_____

_____

_____

BONUS FUN TIME!

Express *alert* with a drawing, or
invent a dictionary-style definition of your own.

escalate

es·ca·late • [Es-kuh-layt] • \ ˈeskə͜ˌlāt \

- verb

    1. to increase in extent, volume, number, amount, or scope

The runners **escalated** their pace until they were basically sprinting!

SYNONYM

ANTONYM

WRITING TIME!
Use *escalate* in an original sentence of your own creation.

BONUS FUN TIME!
Express *escalate* with a drawing, or
invent a dictionary-style definition of your own.

exhaust

ex·haust   •   [ig-zAWst]   •   \ igˈzȯst \

- verb
    1. to use up the whole supply or store of;
    2. to drain (someone) of their physical or mental resources

Playing all day with my two-year-old nephew **exhausts** me.

SYNONYM

ANTONYM

WRITING TIME!
Use *exhaust* in an original sentence of your own creation.

BONUS FUN TIME!
Express *exhaust* with a drawing, or
invent a dictionary-style definition of your own.

scarcity

scar·ci·ty • [skAIRs-uh-tee] • \ ˈsker-sə-tē \

- noun

1. smallness of quantity or number in proportion to need;
2. lack of provisions for the support of life

If we have a **scarcity** of water on our hike, we'll find a spring or lake.

SYNONYM

ANTONYM

WRITING TIME!

Use *scarcity* in an original sentence of your own creation.

BONUS FUN TIME!

Express *scarcity* with a drawing, or
invent a dictionary-style definition of your own.

influence

in·flu·ence   •   [In-floo-uhns]   •   \ ˈinˌflüən(t)s \

- noun

1. the capacity to have an effect on the character, development, or behavior of someone or something, or the effect itself

Gordon's **influence** on me was so strong that I couldn't resist.

SYNONYM

ANTONYM

WRITING TIME!
Use *influence* in an original sentence of your own creation.

BONUS FUN TIME!
Express *influence* with a drawing, or
invent a dictionary-style definition of your own.

superior

su·pe·ri·or • [su-pIR-ee-uhr] • \ su̇-ˈpir-ē-ər \

- adjective
1. of higher degree or rank;
2. of more importance, value, usefulness, or merit

Junior Mints are **superior** to just about every other candy out there.

SYNONYM

ANTONYM

WRITING TIME!
Use *superior* in an original sentence of your own creation.

BONUS FUN TIME!
Express *superior* with a drawing, or
invent a dictionary-style definition of your own.

vertical

ver·ti·cal   •   [vUHR-ti-kuhl]   •   \ ˈvər-ti-kəl \

- adjective
> 1. *perpendicular to the plane of the horizon or to a primary axis;*
> 2. *situated at the highest point*

I have to increase my **vertical** leap if I want to dunk a basketball.

SYNONYM

ANTONYM

WRITING TIME!
Use *vertical* in an original sentence of your own creation.

_____

_____

_____

BONUS FUN TIME!
Express *vertical* with a drawing, or
invent a dictionary-style definition of your own.

survive

sur·vive • [suhr-vIEv] • \ sər-ˈvīv \

- verb
1. *to continue to exist, function, or compete despite something;*
2. *to live beyond the life or existence of : live longer than*

Some tadpoles didn't make it, but the bigger ones **survived**.

SYNONYM

ANTONYM

WRITING TIME!
Use *survive* in an original sentence of your own creation.

_____

_____

_____

BONUS FUN TIME!
Express *survive* with a drawing, or
invent a dictionary-style definition of your own.

SECTION FOUR: WORD REVIEW

Congratulations on learning ten amazing new words! Remember that the whole point of learning new vocabulary is actually to use it, so let's put your new vocabulary to use.

1. Review the words you've learned. Consider what ideas come to mind when you say the words. How about when you read the definitions?
2. Circle at least **two** of your favorites. You'll get to use these when you write your very own story!

anxious —— adjective

1. characterized by extreme uneasiness of mind;
2. characterized by strong earnest desire : ardently wishing

express —— verb

1. to convey (a thought or feeling) in words or by gestures and conduct

alert —— verb

1. to call to a state of readiness

escalate —— verb

1. to increase in extent, volume, number, amount, or scope

exhaust —— verb

1. to use up the whole supply or store of;
2. to drain (someone) of their physical or mental resources

scarcity —— noun

1. smallness of quantity or number in proportion to need;
2. lack of provisions for the support of life

influence —— noun

1. the capacity to have an effect on the character, development, or behavior of someone or something, or the effect itself

superior —— adjective

1. of higher degree or rank;
2. of more importance, value, usefulness, or merit

vertical —— adjective

1. perpendicular to the plane of the horizon or to a primary axis;
2. situated at the highest point

survive —— verb

1. to continue to exist, function, or compete despite something;
2. to live beyond the life or existence of : live longer than

STORY FOUR

1. List the words you've chosen:

_____

2. Write a story that incorporates all of your chosen words. If you can't think of anything to write about, consider these suggestions:

   - **Write a story that takes place on the last day of school.**
   - **Write a story in which the main character has a pet spider big enough to walk on a leash.**

Title: _____

_____

_____

_____

_____

_____

_____

_____

Caption: _____

_____

_____

_____

_____

_____

_____

_____

_____

Wonderful Words for Fifth Grade Vocabulary & Writing Workbook ©2021 Grammaropolis LLC

SECTION FIVE: WORD PREVIEW
Welcome to your ten new favorite words!

When you encounter a new word, take a moment to consider what it might mean.
1. Think about the word and circle what part of speech you think it is.
   *(Many words can act as more than one part of speech, depending on how they're used in the sentence, **so only choose one part of speech below**.)*
2. Come up with a brief definition of the word in the part of speech you've chosen. It doesn't have to be the *correct* definition—just do your best.

horizontal
Part of Speech: noun   verb   adjective

Definition:_____

_____

primary
Part of Speech: noun   verb   adjective

Definition:_____

_____

recent
Part of Speech: noun   verb   adjective

Definition:_____

_____

entertain
Part of Speech: noun   verb   adjective

Definition:_____

_____

gist
Part of Speech: noun   verb   adjective

Definition:_____

_____

edible
Part of Speech: noun   verb   adjective

Definition:_____

_____

competition
Part of Speech: noun   verb   adjective

Definition:_____

_____

fragile
Part of Speech: noun   verb   adjective

Definition:_____

_____

disaster
Part of Speech: noun   verb   adjective

Definition:_____

_____

baggage
Part of Speech: noun   verb   adjective

Definition:_____

_____

horizontal

hor·i·zon·tal • [hor-uh-zAHnt-l] • \ ˌhôrəˈzän(t)l \

- adjective

   1. parallel to the plane of the horizon : at right angles to the vertical

A glass won't slide off the edge of a perfectly **horizontal** table.

SYNONYM

ANTONYM

WRITING TIME!
Use *horizontal* in an original sentence of your own creation.

BONUS FUN TIME!
Express *horizontal* with a drawing, or
invent a dictionary-style definition of your own.

primary

pri·ma·ry • [prIE-mair-ee] • \ ˈprī-ˌmer-ē \

- **adjective**
    1. *first in rank or importance;*
    2. *first in order of time or development*

    The **primary** reason for having a birthday party is to eat cake.

SYNONYM

ANTONYM

WRITING TIME!
Use *primary* in an original sentence of your own creation.

BONUS FUN TIME!
Express *primary* with a drawing, or
invent a dictionary-style definition of your own.

recent

re·cent   •   [rEE-s-nt]   •   \ ˈrēs(ə)nt \

- adjective

    1. having happened, begun, or been done not long ago or not long before

The **recent** storm knocked out our electricity, so we're using candles.

SYNONYM

ANTONYM

WRITING TIME!
Use *recent* in an original sentence of your own creation.

BONUS FUN TIME!
Express *recent* with a drawing, or
invent a dictionary-style definition of your own.

entertain

en·ter·tain   •   [en-tuhr-tAYn]   •   \ ˌen(t)ərˈtān \

- verb

1. to cause the time to pass pleasantly for (someone) : amuse;

2. to show hospitality to : provide for the needs of (a guest)

Last night we **entertained** each other by telling funny jokes.

SYNONYM

ANTONYM

WRITING TIME!

Use *entertain* in an original sentence of your own creation.

BONUS FUN TIME!

Express *entertain* with a drawing, or
invent a dictionary-style definition of your own.

gist

gist   •   [jlst]   •   \ ˈjist \

- noun

1. the main point or material part (as of a question or debate)

Do you understand the **gist** of the lesson, or do you need more help?

SYNONYM

ANTONYM

WRITING TIME!
Use *gist* in an original sentence of your own creation.

BONUS FUN TIME!
Express *gist* with a drawing, or
invent a dictionary-style definition of your own.

edible

ed·i·ble   •   [Ed-uh-buhl]   •   \ ˈedəbəl \

- adjective

1. suitable by nature for use as food especially for human beings

Those mushrooms are not **edible**, so please don't eat them!

SYNONYM

ANTONYM

WRITING TIME!
Use *edible* in an original sentence of your own creation.

_____

_____

_____

BONUS FUN TIME!
Express *edible* with a drawing, or
invent a dictionary-style definition of your own.

competition

com·pe·ti·tion • [kahm-puh-tIsh-uhn] • \ ˌkämpəˈtiSH(ə)n \

- noun

1. *the activity or condition of competing;*
2. *the opposition in a contest*

Dayton entered the **discus** competition because it sounded fun.

SYNONYM

ANTONYM

WRITING TIME!
Use *competition* in an original sentence of your own creation.

BONUS FUN TIME!
Express *competition* with a drawing, or
invent a dictionary-style definition of your own.

fragile

frag·ile   •   [frAj-uhl]   •   \ ˈfra-jəl \

- adjective

1. easily broken or destroyed

That action figure is extremely **fragile**, so please handle it with care.

SYNONYM

ANTONYM

WRITING TIME!
Use *fragile* in an original sentence of your own creation.

BONUS FUN TIME!
Express *fragile* with a drawing, or
invent a dictionary-style definition of your own.

disaster

di·sas·ter • [di-zAs-tuhr] • \ dəˈzastər \

- noun

1. *a sudden calamitous event producing great material damage, loss, and distress*

Hurricane Harvey was a horrible **disaster** for the city of Houston.

SYNONYM

ANTONYM

WRITING TIME!
Use *disaster* in an original sentence of your own creation.

BONUS FUN TIME!
Express *disaster* with a drawing, or
invent a dictionary-style definition of your own.

baggage

bag·gage • [bAgIj] • \ ˈba-gij \

- noun
1. personal belongings packed in suitcases for traveling;
2. past experiences or long-held ideas regarded as burdens

Make sure to have your **baggage** with you at all times during the trip.

SYNONYM

ANTONYM

WRITING TIME!
Use *baggage* in an original sentence of your own creation.

BONUS FUN TIME!
Express *baggage* with a drawing, or
invent a dictionary-style definition of your own.

Section Five: Word Review

Congratulations on learning ten amazing new words! Remember that the whole point of learning new vocabulary is actually to use it, so let's put your new vocabulary to use.

1. Review the words you've learned. Consider what ideas come to mind when you say the words. How about when you read the definitions?
2. Circle at least **two** of your favorites. You'll get to use these when you write your very own story!

horizontal — adjective
1. parallel to the plane of the horizon : at right angles to the vertical

primary — adjective
1. first in rank or importance;
2. first in order of time or development

recent — adjective
1. having happened, begun, or been done not long ago or not long before

entertain — verb
1. to cause the time to pass pleasantly for (someone) : amuse;
2. to show hospitality to : provide for the needs of (a guest)

gist — noun
1. the main point or material part (as of a question or debate)

edible — adjective
1. suitable by nature for use as food especially for human beings

competition — noun
1. the activity or condition of competing;
2. the opposition in a contest

fragile — adjective
1. easily broken or destroyed

disaster — noun
1. a sudden calamitous event producing great material damage, loss, and distress

baggage — noun
1. personal belongings packed in suitcases for traveling;
2. past experiences or long-held ideas regarded as burdens

Story Five

1. List the words you've chosen:

_____

2. Write a story that incorporates all of your chosen words. If you can't think of anything to write about, consider these suggestions:
   - Write a story in about getting the chance to fix your greatest regret.
   - Write a story in which the main character is a circus clown.

Title: _____

_____

_____

_____

_____

_____

_____

_____

_____

_____

_____

_____

_____

_____

Caption: _____

_____

_____

_____

_____

_____

_____

_____

_____

_____

Section Six: Word Preview
Welcome to your ten new favorite words!

When you encounter a new word, take a moment to consider what it might mean.

1. Think about the word and circle what part of speech you think it is. *(Many words can act as more than one part of speech, depending on how they're used in the sentence, **so only choose one part of speech below.**)*

2. Come up with a brief definition of the word in the part of speech you've chosen. It doesn't have to be the *correct* definition—just do your best.

abolish
Part of Speech: noun   verb   adjective

Definition:_____

_____

equivalent
Part of Speech: noun   verb   adjective

Definition:_____

_____

frequent
Part of Speech: noun   verb   adjective

Definition:_____

_____

generosity
Part of Speech: noun   verb   adjective

Definition:_____

_____

navigate
Part of Speech: noun   verb   adjective

Definition:_____

_____

conclude
Part of Speech: noun   verb   adjective

Definition:_____

_____

venture
Part of Speech: noun   verb   adjective

Definition:_____

_____

considerable
Part of Speech: noun   verb   adjective

Definition:_____

_____

plentiful
Part of Speech: noun   verb   adjective

Definition:_____

_____

tension
Part of Speech: noun   verb   adjective

Definition:_____

_____

abolish

abol·ish • [uh-bAHl-ish] • \ ə-ˈbä-lish \

- verb

  1. *to do away with wholly (as in laws, customs, institutions, or traditions)*

Mrs. Dorman wants to **abolish** the word "failure" from her classroom.

SYNONYM

ANTONYM

WRITING TIME!

Use *abolish* in an original sentence of your own creation.

BONUS FUN TIME!

Express *abolish* with a drawing, or
invent a dictionary-style definition of your own.

equivalent

equiv·a·lent • [i-kwIv-uh-luhnt] • \ əˈkwiv(ə)lənt \

- adjective

1. *equal in value, amount, function, or meaning*

Jorge and I traded **equivalent** amounts of chocolate with each other.

SYNONYM

ANTONYM

WRITING TIME!

Use *equivalent* in an original sentence of your own creation.

BONUS FUN TIME!

Express *equivalent* with a drawing, or
invent a dictionary-style definition of your own.

frequent

fre·quent • [frEE-kwuhnt] • \ ˈfrē-kwənt \

- adjective

1. *occurring or done on many occasions, in many cases, or in quick succession*

Being a **frequent** napper means that you nap all the time.

SYNONYM

ANTONYM

WRITING TIME!

Use *frequent* in an original sentence of your own creation.

BONUS FUN TIME!

Express *frequent* with a drawing, or
invent a dictionary-style definition of your own.

generosity

gen·er·os·i·ty • [jen-uhr-rAHs-uh-tee] • \ ˌjenəˈräsədē \

- noun
1. *the quality of being kind and generous;*
2. *the quality of having abundance*

Lyall displayed tremendous **generosity** when she shared her donut.

SYNONYM

ANTONYM

WRITING TIME!
Use *generosity* in an original sentence of your own creation.

BONUS FUN TIME!
Express *generosity* with a drawing, or
invent a dictionary-style definition of your own.

navigate

nav·i·gate   •   [nAv-uh-gayt]   •   \ ˈna-və-ˌgāt \

- verb
>*1. to direct one's course through any medium;*
>*2. to go from one place to another by water : sail*

With the help of a good map, you can **navigate** through any city.

SYNONYM

ANTONYM

WRITING TIME!
Use *navigate* in an original sentence of your own creation.

_____

_____

_____

BONUS FUN TIME!
Express *navigate* with a drawing, or
invent a dictionary-style definition of your own.

conclude

con·clude • [kuhn-klOOd] • \ kən-ˈklüd \

- verb
1. *to bring to an end;*
2. *to reach a final determination or judgment about*

The politician **concluded** her speech with a story about leadership.

SYNONYM

ANTONYM

WRITING TIME!
Use *conclude* in an original sentence of your own creation.

BONUS FUN TIME!
Express *conclude* with a drawing, or
invent a dictionary-style definition of your own.

venture

ven·ture   •   [vEn-chuhr]   •   \ ˈven(t)-shər \

> **- noun**
>
> *1. a journey or undertaking involving chance, risk, or danger*
>
> Starting a lemonade stand is hard, but it's a **venture** worth taking.

SYNONYM

ANTONYM

WRITING TIME!
Use *venture* in an original sentence of your own creation.

BONUS FUN TIME!
Express *venture* with a drawing, or
invent a dictionary-style definition of your own.

considerable

con·sid·er·a·ble • [kuhn-sɪd-uhr-ruh-buhl] • \ kənˈsid(ə)rəb(ə)l \

- adjective
 1. *notably large in size, amount, or extent;*
 2. *having merit or distinction*

I got a **considerable** amount of sand in my shoes at the beach today.

SYNONYM	ANTONYM

WRITING TIME!
Use *considerable* in an original sentence of your own creation.

_____

_____

_____

BONUS FUN TIME!
Express *considerable* with a drawing, or
invent a dictionary-style definition of your own.

plentiful

plen·ti·ful • [plEn-ti-fuhl] • \ ˈplentəfəl \

- adjective

1. containing or yielding great quantities : fruitful

The orchard gave us a **plentiful** crop of delicious apples this year.

SYNONYM	ANTONYM

WRITING TIME!
Use *plentiful* in an original sentence of your own creation.

BONUS FUN TIME!
Express *plentiful* with a drawing, or
invent a dictionary-style definition of your own.

tension

ten·sion • [tEn-shuhn] • \ ˈten(t)-shən \

- noun
> 1. the state of being stretched tight;
> 2. mental or emotional strain

If that guitar string is under too much **tension**, it might snap.

SYNONYM

ANTONYM

WRITING TIME!
Use *tension* in an original sentence of your own creation.

BONUS FUN TIME!
Express *tension* with a drawing, or
invent a dictionary-style definition of your own.

Section Six: Word Review

Congratulations on learning ten amazing new words! Remember that the whole point of learning new vocabulary is actually to use it, so let's put your new vocabulary to use.

1. Review the words you've learned. Consider what ideas come to mind when you say the words. How about when you read the definitions?
2. Circle at least **two** of your favorites. You'll get to use these when you write your very own story!

abolish ──── verb
1. *to do away with wholly (as in laws, customs, institutions, or traditions)*

equivalent ──── adjective
1. *equal in value, amount, function, or meaning*

frequent ──── adjective
1. *occurring or done on many occasions, in many cases, or in quick succession*

generosity ──── noun
1. *the quality of being kind and generous;*
2. *the quality of having abundance*

navigate ──── verb
1. *to direct one's course through any medium;*
2. *to go from one place to another by water : sail*

conclude ──── verb
1. *to bring to an end;*
2. *to reach a final determination or judgment about*

venture ──── noun
1. *a journey or undertaking involving chance, risk, or danger*

considerable ── adjective
1. *notably large in size, amount, or extent;*
2. *having merit or distinction*

plentiful ──── adjective
1. *containing or yielding great quantities : fruitful*

tension ──── noun
1. *the state of being stretched tight;*
2. *mental or emotional strain*

STORY SIX

1. List the words you've chosen:

_____

2. Write a story that incorporates all of your chosen words. If you can't think of anything to write about, consider these suggestions:
   - Write a story that takes place entirely in a grocery store.
   - Write a story about finally standing up to a bully.

Title: _____

_____

_____

_____

_____

_____

_____

_____

Wonderful Words for Fifth Grade Vocabulary & Writing Workbook ©2021 Grammaropolis LLC

Caption: _____

_____

_____

_____

_____

_____

_____

_____

_____

Wonderful Words for Fifth Grade Vocabulary & Writing Workbook ©2021 Grammaropolis LLC

INDEX OF WORDS USED